IN WINTER
I BURN POEMS

IN WINTER I BURN POEMS

POEMS

Diana Lischer

GREEN WRITERS PRESS *Brattleboro, Vermont*

Printed in the United States

10 9 8 7 6 5 4 3 2 1

Green Writers Press is a Vermont-based publisher whose mission is to spread a message of hope and renewal through the words and images we publish. Throughout we will adhere to our commitment to preserving and protecting the natural resources of the earth. To that end, a percentage of our proceeds will be donated to environmental activist groups. Green Writers Press gratefully acknowledges support from individual donors, friends, and readers to help support the environment and our publishing initiative.

Green Writers Press

Giving Voice to Writers & Artists Who Will Make the World a Better Place

Green Writers Press | Brattleboro, Vermont

www.greenwriterspress.com

ISBN: 979-8-9985170-6-8

PRINTED ON 100% PCW RECYCLED PAPER BY BOOKMOBILE.
BASED IN MINNEAPOLIS, MINNESOTA, BOOKMOBILE BEGAN AS A DESIGN AND TYPESETTING PRODUCTION HOUSE IN 1982, AND STARTED OFFERING PRINT SERVICES IN 1996.
BOOKMOBILE IS RUN ON 100% WIND- AND SOLAR-POWERED CLEAN ENERGY.

Contents

WINTER

SPRING

SUMMER

FALL

WINTER

In Winter I Burn Poems

My poems are quilts
sewn with imaginary threads,
piecing the red of joy, the blue of love lost,
gathered in my lap of comfort.

I frame my life in soft-worn panels
of hard-won cloth,
cross-stitched hope
and the *Wild Geese* of desire.

My poems are lovers
for my cold bones:
chilled ivory needles, pins of pain
sharpened by the gold teeth of dogs.

My words are comforters:
I tie the seams and ragged edges
with calico bits of dreams
in the night of *Ohio Stars*.

I take my quilts
from their winter storage of paper
and cast them as kindling to the flame,
banking the embers with their pale skins.

Cat-eyed coals,
they sizzle with tears,
joyous and painful.

In winter, I burn poems.

This Woodstove

This woodstove,
it is my heart—

the one I lost years ago
and come to this hearth
to claim—

Reclaim, this ironclad organ
and cleanse my soul in its fire,
where the light is so fierce,
I forget my sorrow.

Only this death of the past,
I hunger for in my stove-hood,
baking that last vestige
of coal to ash.

I have no voice to cry the dark away,
but the warmth of my firebox
cradles my soul in breath, hissing—

the dark oaken tree gone up in smoke.

Soapstone

Soapstone,
How does your softness last?
Time speckles you with green secrets
From nights when you were stolen,
Your sightless quarries blasted
By frowning men,
Who did not care for your beauty?

But hoarded you in chalky piles of talc.
They sawed you
Into chunky pillows of cotton stone
To warm the beds of Boston spinsters.

Loyal heat,
You hold my winter in radiant chambers,
Iron my toes with your warmth and kindness.

The covers smother us like lovers too warm
To strike a light together,
And subdued by radiation
Of arches on supple stone.

Soft as powdered babies,
You, I surround
With aching feet brutalized by boots
Worn from dancing in Grange halls.

Dependable,
You wait on the crest of my blackened stove,
Peering from your square-rootedness.

Rivers have rubbed your edges
From infamous days,
Offer me hard love from soft rock.

Cambridgeport, Vermont

The neon Budweiser sign glares red
from the sleeping storefront
on this October night,
as owls echo each other
and coyotes hunt the moon
through the lost windows
of the woolen mill ruins.

Vaguely crackles early flames of history
in the guttural run of Weaver Brook,
rolling beneath arches,
where power once reigned
to run the mill.

Past old Doc Weaver's homestead
scrolls the water,
which has seen the land
swallowed by swollen rivers
and crops collapsed
in broken furrows.

Now,
Weaver's place is a clinic
for Model-T's
overhauled by collectors
of past glory,
when automobiles drank
petrol by the glassful.

Weaver Brook flows past
the blacksmith's house.

His iron will
drips strong and black
in the doors—
in latches and hinges
is known the master
of the anvil.

The acid of horseshoeing
has spat
its pocked signature
in the soapstone sink
sitting silent and knowing
in the kitchen window.

Square-headed nails,
nearly squared doorways
mark legends
of plain talking
and straight foresight
to the things that last
beyond each planed board
the doors crossed by the faith
of Christian belief
in the virtue of sweat
from brow and forearm.

The houses were raised
from the ledges
and lean against the wildness of night,
each blessed
by stone cellars
steady in shifting tides.

River and wind
cannot tear the memory
from sill and shingle,
joist and plank,
from stone and mortar.

Cambridgeport, Vermont—
stubborn in spirit
despite the sale of its church,
passage of its mill—
the silence
of its soapstone quarries.

The lights still burn quick
as candles in a storm
in these homes of hearty souls,
who still farm and plod along
with Weaver Brook,
as she mulls
over ancient rock
worn in talc and blood,
reminds us to praise stone and water.

To a Gravestone

"Comfort Thrasher – a soldier in the year of 1812, and wife, Anna"

The crow in the elm asks:
How did you survive to 1871?
Rheumatism your only companion,
token of the bloodbath of brothers in the South?

Did you hide slaves beneath the Cambridgeport Hotel,
the tunnel teeming with black bodies,
running like molasses to the woolen mill
in the night when the big dipper starred?

Did you cut soapstone from Grafton quarries
for bed warmers shipped to Boston spinsters?
Was your hearing a jangle of ringing
from the thunder of the dynamite?

Did you comfort your dear wife, Anna,
had she "*gone to meet her loved ones,*"
as she lay on her death bed under a quilt
pieced with golden rings for her wedding day?

No children to comfort you in your 84th year,
but you harvested your sweet corn memories
when you fed the heifers like they were your own flesh
and their milk gave you comfort and butter.

The sugar from the bush of maples
sweetened the sour days into gold,
stuck to your brain with sticky recollections:
buckets of sap water quenching an old man's thirst.

And dearest Anna kept time with her knitting,
piecing blocks for a neighbor's birthing,
a quilt for a wedding, a shroud for a family,
all work is love and comfort to the one who toils.

And through war and death, birth and marriage,
it is all one ball of wax molded in red falling leaves
each lick of rain on headstones softens the years
into marble weepings of gray-striped stone.

If you listen carefully,
the ghosts whisper like bees from a hive of graves.

Writing in his Heart's Domain

Robert Frost Homestead, Shaftsbury, Vermont

Writing in his heart's domain:
past stone walls tumbled down to sod
where years of sheep and cows have lain,
where horses' hooves have trod.

The land has lost its bag of grain,
the years have dumped their load
of timbered time and heart's refrain,
the trail of poems told.

Writing in his heart's domain:
a hawk flies from its folds
of wing, caught shy in sun's last flame,
the tale of verse is told.

Along the wind in snow and rain,
his treasures lay like gold;
the stone embedded in the train,
the line of pine planted in the cold.

Writing in his heart's domain:
within the apple's wood
rings of sonnets softly strain
and whisper as they should.

In spring, the light is tame,
his chickens gone for good.
Another rock is just the same
as every other wood.

Whose woods are these, I think I know,
betrays the warmth of this domain.
He shared them with a heart of gold,
a lover's quarrel with the world remains.

Wherein, *whose woods are these,* is plain,
the invitation to obtain,
to bid and join his heart's domain,
both cow and man who knew,

the soft refrain, and lowly prayer,
a fleeting, *you come too.*

Madonna of Sarajevo

Madonna of Sarajevo,
only the Carpathians remain
as truth is swallowed by mountain caves
and forests are auctioned.

You sink to your knees in Slavic Bosnia
sliced with hunger
and the traveling shows of war.

You travel the bones of headless borders
to rescue ghosts
who dance shoeless in the snow.

Thirst calls: drink here
from a well so clear that memory
held between lips of three centuries
pours the chill of Black Forest into your veins.

Your face,
your forests,
your children rooted in bold-branching time,
grow a conscience as strong as oak.

Angel of Silesia,
you have whittled a stubborn doll of grace,
the only hope,
this token held in your hand.

Black Bear

Black Bear,

I taste your honey breath
in the shadows,
melting into obsidian night.

I dream your rough fur
smelling of heather and peat,
your moist mouth
at my neck.

Let us dance a circle
in a crystal sky,
the stars, my crown,
and you,
my arch.

Take me to your heart,
your cave,
your burial ground—

Let me walk in your path
of soft shadows.

SPRING

Spring Runs Blind

Spring runs blind beneath ice banks of West River.
The land longs for itself, it percolates imprisoned,
a gift in a box to be unwrapped by starlight.
Spring tracks the Abenaki Moose Moon,
coming to a theatre near you, free for the viewing.
We stretch to a third year of vacant dreams,
holding onto one more day until, like the Spring,
we emerge free from our shackles of Winter,
the community invasion, the source of our discontent.
We refuse to seek comfort in hibernation,
to be like Bear in our backyard isolation installed
until Spring, until freedom,
until release from the time of Corona.
The halo of the moon stalks us as in a dream,
a corona in the kingdom of the here and now.
We learn, whether we want to or not,
to be kind.

Green

I crawl through the cracks
between stone and ice
on knees worn like beach shell.

Quickly, I see light from above,
a sprinkling of sun
in my eye.

The glassy graze of rain drops
clink on the pebbled face
of these prison walls.

The blue is a bugle for my soul,
as the tunnel narrows against my green ribs,
I scrape my tender thighs.

I ache with each inch of my cells
as squeezing my trunk
through the eye of a needle.

Ah, an air pocket!
And breathing is loose
like champagne through an ice cap.

And bursting into scented air,
I shoot myself, breaking the sound barrier
between earth and sky.

If you were not asleep in your daydreams,
you would hear my cry
and taste my green.

Iris Cristata

Irises in dead leaves,
one and all, we are
bursting in dank pools,
feathered faces to the light,
shy/bold in our turning,
the season rises purple to the sky.

Out of the hunkering of winter
buds tingle and flush,
straining to taste the frosted warmth
blaring from the East
pelting robins and their worms,
with laser tom-foolery.

Blue tongues and violet hoods,
we unfurl in wet, new grass
and shun the snow
left leering on the mountain,
bleary eyes of slush,
and gray-hearted mud
slides along the roadside.

Blink, and we are gone.
Withered wicks of blue soot,
flames as temporary as spring,
the tease of April
in one exhalation
of indigo.

Ice Islands

In April: Islands of ice,
and the sand is banked
by swollen fingers
of a green and hungry river.

The vibration strokes the stones
of the river's bed,
and hordes the bracken treasures
of a year of stormings.

Ice reclines in dirty gauntness
where a beaver scavenges the bones of a birch
to fasten a new shelter, the old shorn
by the passion of melting mountaintops.

The ice islands give little comfort
to crows stalking in hunger
the pump and darting shadows
among the skulking, wet rocks.

Only ice
feeds the trout streaming,
the river flinging her torso,
raising her reedy mane of witchgrass:

As cube by cube,
the level of chill in the heart rises,
aching for a bridge, any old log,
to touch another island only a body away.

In April: we are trapped
On ice islands,
Worked by the water
In frantic sculpture:

Bumping ourselves against other islands,
freezer-burned and ice bound,
slipping, ever so slightly,
then crashing into a calculating river.

Drinking in the Rain

I could talk about the rain,
but you would have to listen
yourself.

It speaks the language
of the self:
aloneness,
one with the softness of earth,
yet found in excess along the pages of leaves,
under the wings of mayflies
who stagger in the tragedy of unraveling spring.

It is lost in trout rendezvous,
percolating to the sponge of the land,
to secret caverns of memory
when drops fell
as drums on a tin roof,
the farmhouse shuddered with thunder
and glowed with the jagged grace of electricity.

What shock
to soak the earth in its wet glory
where tears seep between
rips in the ozone;
tap, taps a reminder:
that to stand
alone
against the strident song of calamity,
is to
drink in the rain.

Shoveling Dirt

Cool earth meets hovering air.
The dirt pile grows high enough to shade
my puppy, whose muddy snout snuggles into damp
  shadows along the garden wall.
My shovel wearies, and I rest on its wooden handle
  rubbed shiny by a thousand gardens.

Legions of lupines and digitalis pose for their weeding
  and watering
along the stone wall built by Italian masons, who
  christened this farm with their sweat,
and blessed these barns with steady footings of
  chiseled, gray slate.

The earth whispers of other farm women, their herbs
  planted close to the hearth—
their breath light as snow on an early spring day such
  as this.
They pinched parsley, sage and rue for various
  purposes- colds, insomnia—
to conjure teas and broths made in heaven for earthly
  cares.

The shovel bites into sods stillborn along the rocks
  and bearded iris—
another chomp of its blade severs the clay near
  burgeoning hollyhocks, their umbrella leaves open
  to the black flies of May.
Another stitch into the lattice of witchgrass, and I am
  nearly done.

Dirt clods drop like wet boots, and the grass recoils
like an emerald mattress.
The next shovel-full brims with treasure: the gold
spotlights of a salamander
glistens and I lower this rare piece of garden jewelry.
It slithers back into a crevice of stone.

I hold my breath as if, for a thousand Sundays, I rest
against this shovel.
I give thanks to the elements, the wind, the rain, the
sun
smiling along the workdays strung like amber beads
of summer.

Morels in May

After May showers, I walk in a whisper,
trying not to disturb the nut-brown morels
I know are squatting like gnomes
beneath umbrellas of leaves under ancient apple trees.

They are dressed in supple, Swiss-cheese coats,
their accordion bodies hunkering down
between earth and apple droppings,
tidying up the leaf mold and herding earthworms.

They are eyeless, and mouthless
but in perpetual petulance.
They are open to the fragrance of apple blossoms
and the vicissitudes of the orchard in spring.

They hide cleverly in the dank of apple shadow,
but if I call them with an open heart
they tip their caps, holy and solemn,
presenting themselves to my believing eye.

With open lungs and corrugated hearts,
these trusting fungi push through leaf pack,
debris of a weary winter,
morels stand naked in May's warm wonder.

Jubilant and eager to breathe again,
they hide in paper layers
of last year's harvest of apple leaves,
an envelope to be torn by battalions of morels.

The thought of their presence delights me,

even as frustration leaves me with no choice
but to call them by name:
"Here morel, where are you, Mr. Morel?"

And the apple trees
are shelters of silence,
guarding their orchard sanctuary,
lording over their turf of brown leaves.

To pick morels,
you must quiet yourself,
call them by name
and politely request them to show themselves.
For if you do not believe in them,
they will not let you find them.
They rely on you to hurry by
not noticing how plumply they sit.

Like Buddhas beneath the oldest stand of trees,
they have been awakening each spring
from a deep, dark leaf-bound sleep.
and you have not stopped to see.

They really are there all along,
raising the roof of their paper-thin huts,
their leaf shields protecting them from harm,
and from human harvest.

They are tricksters who adapt
like all fungi to their surroundings,
quietly mocking you
when you walk by them with unseeing eyes.

They can only be known
to those who truly believe
that they can converse
with gnomes beneath apple trees.

Otherwise,
they languish another season,
sending out spores for future morels
to grow uninterrupted among the apples.

As come next May,
the first warm showers sing
over the halo of orchard blossom,
and awaken all the gnomes who slumber there.

Spirit of the Red Hawk

Spirit of the Red Hawk:
You dance in the heartbeat of storms,
stark-eyed and razor-winged,
licking hot vapors in the snow.

Like the breath of hallowed smoke,
You shadow the salted firmament
with fire and feather,
bones whistling on funeral wings.

Eagle of the Eastern sun-script:
arrow-tongued and perverse,
you shred the flesh with flints
of Truth and seasoned Passion.

Keening—
        Careening—
                Rising—
                        Screeching—

You straddle the human desert,
talons splayed,
askance—
bold with stolen blood.

Your honest hunger
shrieks a carrion sacrifice,
the heart's desire
for its own consumption:

Bright Cannibal of Angels!

Triangle Shirtwaist Fire

New York City, March 25, 1911

A drab coat of New York night
hems in the wanton, waning light.
Singers clack like laying hens,
their bobbins bob, their needles mend.

The bell buttons down the day,
keys jangle past the time to stay.
A call rings through, a fire brews—
smoke drifts along the seam of gray.

Sarah cries: "the doors are locked!"
She strangles in thin air.
The swelter stalks in heavy knots,
it snakes along the pin-lit stair.

Young women falling from the sky
aglow in blackened rain;
with flapping skirts and hose they fly
in raven screams of flame.

Mere spider-nets, the men hand-hold.
They do not know the laws
of the physics of objects bowled
along a sheet of gauze.

The three entwine as lovers,
shoot like arrows through the silk.
The cough of shredded flowers,
they spill like mother's milk.

The earth resounds with every crash,
such beauty have they broke.
The idol of the hourglass
baptized in soot and smoke.

Factory girls with shoveled hearts,
track the company's unholy slaughter;
a burial fit for cast-off parts:
the grave of the unknown daughter.

SUMMER

Wind on Sand

The wind whispers to her body
from the sea of childhood,
the taunts of wind on sand,
hands of breath on pearl skin.

The body is shed like a crab's shell
at low tide, discarded in slick sand,
the photograph stills to a mere wash
of scattered light
on endlessly sweeping sand.

All of her life swims away to the open sea.
The child in the buttercup suit and lemon hair
cradles a shell to listen,
inhales the future hiss
of Eros.

If Margaret Sanger Sang a Song

An Adult Nursery Rhyme

If Margaret Sanger Sang a Song,
she'd sing a song to me,
she'd sing a song to you, my love,
of time's equality.

That men and women are one clay
with tidal tribulations,
by dusk and dawn in lusty play
and primal jubilations.

Their arctic bodies seek the poles:
lost conflicts, dark and bright,
a sweet commingling of souls:
wet and warm, loose and tight.

Seasons reel, the bones remain,
the body eats itself.
Vultures covet and spiders claim
the debris of winter's wealth.

With tender flesh of summer light
and brittle hands of gray,
each man and woman stands the night,
and scores the face of day.

If Margaret Sanger sang a song,
she'd sing a song to me,
she'd sing a song to you, my love,
of time's equality.

I Lost My Hunger for Fishing

I lost my hunger a long time ago
for fishing in the hush of twilight;
the sweetness of life too much to bear,
to hook the soft mouth,
the eyes glazed in surprise,
the silver tail tarnishing before my eyes.

I lost the sweetness a long time ago
of gently rocking boats,
pulling oars in the salt of fog
my father's voice, his hands a wooden memory,
lost on a shelf of books.

I lost my innocence a long time ago,
the cool hush of death sweet on my neck,
the ocean fishing for my soul
as I fished once
in Newfoundland along the coast,
the cod grieving for me as it bled.

I lost my hunger for fishing a long time ago,
the squid screaming in the night,
the ink, the blinding florescence of their skin
cannot be repeated in the song
of the silver net I cling to in my sea,
the voyage not quite over.

The Kingfisher

The kingfisher carries clarity on her back;
the precision of her flight holds
the thought of fishing in each feather
bound by the sinew of her breast:

The true collaboration of heart and soul on the wing.

Truly, her wind dance is intrepid,
a stab through the summer
air above river,
the sharp arrow of purpose
to the task of seeking silver prey
on this silver dollar day,
when light flies, too, and hovers
a shiny task in green and blue reflections:

the clear breath of summer after a rain,
the cleansing weight of it all.

Pearls are crushed into sand
left glinting on the neck of the river:

the point where land and water
tell one another they are separate,
though they ache for each other's embrace
of bubble and sand.

But the kingfisher cuts through the illusions,
navigates herself through the clarity.
She does not share the same thoughts
as the river and earth.

Hers is the clear conviction
that the space of her time is limitless,
and in so seeing the door open,
flies clean as an arrow through it
breaking the warp of water.

Allen's Blue Heron

As you lay dying,

I saw a blue heron.

A slate sculpture arcing heaven-bound
startled by my appearance
among the loose strife of late summer:

the flowers I planted when we still lived together,
those wild pink wands I picked for many a wedding.

But not for ours.

The heron distracted me with her clean blueness,
her sleek plumage like a cloudy day,
hovering over a stormy seascape.

The time escapes me when I felt such wonder,
on this day,
when all I think of is you
in your broken-winged body.

I see the grace of the heron,
a reflection of your spirit in one good eye.

The vision of you flying,
your great blue spirit
chasing frogs among the golden lilies
like chalices open to the sun,
drinking the humid air.

The heron pierces her body
through a future only she can see.

Her arrowed mouth knows her mark,
a calligraphy of feathers.

Her neck is as serpentine as the path
we have walked along together,
soon to part.

She is luck incarnate,
home to all that the heart can retain.

Hereafter and always
she returns to this spot,
year upon layer of year,
to ruffle the wind along Weaver Brook,
while she empties her watery heart
into the wet lands along Beauty Road.

Happily may I walk.
May it be beautiful before me.
May it be beautiful behind me.
May it be beautiful above me.
May it be beautiful all around me.
In beauty it is finished.
Ho.

(Navajo prayer)

Compost

Whenever I bury compost
in my garden
at night
by flashlight,
I imagine a horror story;
my ideas are strange.

Perhaps the blue, cloudy mold
or the shocking salmon-orange
gives rise to this atrocity
of thought.

As I dig in the earth,
crawling with venous worms,
I see a doll-like hand
unearthed buy my spade.

I hear the whispered scratch
of neighbors peering over fences:
I just know she's burying a body
in that garden of hers.

My ideas are strange
whenever I bury compost
in my garden
at night
by flashlight
since I buried my placenta:
the blue vein of umbilical cord
in its maroon worm disguise.

The soil is so fertile now,
safe as a womb.
It's been long enough now
to grow a baby under there.

Red Poppies

How you ladies flare,
trumpet flame in my eye,
the absence of pale.

Behold my adoration!

My oriental ladies,
dark-eyed and poised,
you bow at the porch stair,
dance on the wind.

Take me in your geisha arms,
waltz me away to China
back to your cardinal fields
of red-beating hearts.

Tres Gladiolas Rojas

Tres gladiolas rojas:

Three red gladiolas
The Father, The Son, The Holy Mother of God,
let's not forget the mother.

She cleaved her own body
like a rotten melon
into two sideshows:

Woman and Man.

Woman, she cloistered
with the blood of innocents,
rendered the sky vermilion with her sex,
a sponge for all agony!

Man, she sanctified for centuries;
she serves gladly this place of mangos,
where the elite smiles of dogs
market this Mexican mirage.

In the copious blessing of gladiolas,
she blooms scarlet tears
for The Sun, The Moon
and the Holy Summer of Day.

In the Square, Patzcuaro

In the square,
I reach for light—
Patzcuaro air along the night of my quest
for strong and Mexican themes.

In the square,
wind-stapled clouds plait the ceiling of the sky,
while coyotes wait for kindness, appealing
to their crowds of trickster schemes.

In the square,
I am strung up like a ham in the market
my silken hair torn from my life
this life of corn, I am an easy target.

In the square,
Patzcuaro stretches for miles of melon color,
serapes hung in artful clatter,
in tones blind and splattered, cloaking no one.

In the square,
no other matter brings us closer
than *Adobe* tiles tied in weather,
roofs guarded better for the proof of atonement.

In the square,
I pray, facing the light and glitter,
it barely stays in quadrants tighter,
than my clay heart racing the locomotion of the
marketplace.

In the square,
Patzcuaro, beware the thinking earth turns green
like an unripe mango pared into syntax,
shrinks me in the lace of sun grown lax and bitter.

In this square,
I would share lemons with the deep sound of sorrow,
these citric lotions would scent my sleep,
and tomorrow, I would not borrow a single *peso* from
you.

In this sacred square,
Patzcuaro, cower and mingle with me, solo and safe
beneath my blanket of stars and laundered dreams,
our sour fruit cannot scar perfect laughter in the arms
of Mexico.

Riding a Bus in Mexico City

I am riding a bus in Mexico City—
green taxis catapult like grasshoppers through a
  labyrinth of asphalt.

We pass *Zapata's* statue
as tall as any building.
Zapata in full regalia: *sombrero y pistoles*,
his horse proud under smoggy skies,
towers over puddles, *agua negra*, a dark mirror.

A pig roots among shallows of soggy trash.
More human detritus perfumed by flies,
left like leaves to curl and fester under sullen air.
Mexican mountains, like sleeping giants,
muse at the centuries passing as heavy books,
pages frightened of their own story.
¿Donde esta Zapata, jefe de los populous?

Children vend from baskets at the tollbooth,
soldiers graze their horses in downtown parks.
The trees strain under the sidewalks,
their roots a fitful dream of concrete ownership.

The bus driver relaxes in the bounce over a sea of grass.
A coffee-scented river rises to the right,
the first movement of a water symphony
played out in prelude to my pilgrimage to Patzcuaro.

Native farmers study the land after a brief rain,
soft wrinkles on the tragic face of drought.
The land is lonely and barely green.

I imagine a blanket of amber acres welcoming me,
La gringa poetica.
A divine comedy in which white woman
seeks sanctuary among the sullied corridors of
unrestrained mesa,
foundations of a people vanquished.
Some choice between this rabid city left behind
and the polluted Eden of Lake Patzcuaro.

Will *Frida* and *Diego* whisper to me as I walk the
colonial city,
their paint brushes whisking in sequined shadows,
in Arabesque of the light between stars and madness
the disintegrating couple still breathing
seraphim color on canvases of Sierra Nevada night.

Ode to Neruda

Why do trees conceal the splendor of their roots?
¿Por qué los árboles escoden el esplendor de sus raíces?

They hide nothing we do not already know,
how the Earth is soft below,
and the grass clings like a lover.

The roots of all creation linger below
encased by the history of man and woman
written on the wings of prehistoric birds.

We follow the tree line
over every horizon,
forgetting to look to the ground.

Ancestors whisper our names,
but we do not hear
the trees whisper our roots.

They file away the names of troubadours,
gypsies, thieves, poets, philosophers
in the hard safety of caves.

I keep their secrets as I sleep.
Their bones conceal such beauty
beneath these wooden legionnaires,
are we cradled by slender roots of splendor.

Road to Nowhere, Pearce, Arizona

The road snakes through the Coronado Forest of cactus,
the air pregnant with an insect symphony,
waiting for the moon to set,
the sun to finish its ascent.
I hurry my hike knowing that time means heat—
and I know the level of my canteen.

A lone vulture hangs like a wide-winged kite,
with feathers the sun hammers to gold.
I scream at the scavenger, "I'm still moving!"
just to feel some pittance of power,
as I dream through a land no one can own.

Jack rabbits seem to have some place to go,
their mulish ears receive messages from rocks.
They scamper as if late for important dates,
surely not for my entertainment.

I marvel at how a butterfly with paper-thin wings
does not crisp in the dry desert air—
but dances blithely as a beautiful ghost
at a hostile one hundred degrees.

And where is this road going?
And why do I walk it?
It is only there for itself,
and a few ranchers past the gulch.

But here the sounds and sights are all mine.
And a lone cactus glows with magenta blooms,

she speaks to me of beauty incandescent
among dead rocks and graveled sand.

A mountain lion could maul me,
and I would still believe this road goes somewhere,
where life borders death.
It is welcome in its great capacity to charm,
while the noose draws tight as the sun's burning rays.

The Hills of Bisbee

The hills of old Bisbee crouch in the sun,
like watchdogs for my thoughts,
which drift away with the dry wind.

The arid air pulls thoughts out of my brain,
sucking them fast and casting them to the blast
as I wait for each new thought.

To bubble forth like the rivers of water
shadowing the highways,
underground.

But deserts have a way of stealing thoughts—
a meditation of emptiness
just the beauty of blue and grace of sand.

Birds seem to flourish in the high noon sun.
But how they find water
is a mystery.

So, the hills preside in their silent manner,
overseeing their gutted sisters, mountains raped of ore,
and gaping as sacred wounds of history.

Mining in the deepest reality,
the only reason Bisbee exists.
The miners' need for home.

And the hills wait and watch.
Wonder if the miners, the tourists, the artists
will ever leave.

So, the desert keeps drawing their thoughts,
trying to wring us all
of our longings and plans.

Havasuapi Falls

Your misty veil is no mystery after all.
You are the same
as the blood pulsing through these veins
of mine.

We share a common source,
and we take a path down the river.

You arch over the red lip of the canyon,
as if a prayer could save the Earth,
as if Time speaks only in water tongues.

I bring my own prayer to you
to mingle with your turquoise blood,
to carry your jewels with my soul,
embrace the song I carry in my blood to you.

I sing of a time I had almost forgotten,
the place inside my ribs where I am whole,
where joy and sorrow are not a mystery, after all,
and the salty tongues of my tears arch
over the red lip of the canyon of my heart.

FALL

Dreaming of Apples

I dream of apples like some people dream of money,
  love and success.
I desire apples: round, glistening and scented like a
  mountain morning;
a treasure chest of garnets, rubies and golden globes
  of perfect fruit:

Hudson's Golden Gem, Black Oxford, Roxbury Russet.

I dream of apples in the winter, when the world is
  sleeping.
Apples waiting to be pruned before the arrival of the
  carnival of bee hives,
their colored boxes alerting our bear-of-a-dog to
  beware of bees.

I dream of apples in the spring, when apple blossoms
  shiver,
shaking their pink confetti over intoxicated bees
  buzzing,
careening in frantic circuitry of bee-lines to flowers
  soft with pollen.

In summer, the fruit grows plump like well-fed
  children
playing in the sun, cheeks flushed from the exertion
  of ripening.
I dream of their fruition, and my desire for apples
  grows stronger:

Sheep's Nose, Blue Permain, Hubbardston Nonesuch.

I dream that the fruit will bear me to ecstasy—
to pie, perhaps to dream of more voluptuous fruit,
the sweet-tart crunch of taut apple flesh.

In fall, the trees beckon with perfumed temptation,
their apples overbearing, overwhelming:

Holstein, Esopus, Maiden's Blush.

Dreaming of apples—

only harvest means anything to me.

Autumn Apples

I didn't know the generosity of trees
until I discovered the apples in my dooryard—
the trees bent low to the ground,
draped with hundreds of golden globes.

The yellow jackets humming,
like a coffee klatsch
of women who gossip
with morning slung across their eyes.

And the drone of bees
beating their ephemeral wings,
as drunk with ambrosia,
they sip from rotting cups of apple.

Apples clung to childhood
memory like honey
in Autumn sunlight,
still glinting in the eye.

All that gold upon the ground,
a spongy carpet of mash—
the scent of apple death,
a delight to the senses.

Like warm apple wine,
the bouquet of Indian Summer
when the light slants
towards Winter.

But
not
just
yet.

There is an interrupted breath,
as late Fall lingers,
suspended in caramel light
and the soft cider scent of apples
falling
down.

Where did the Wishing Go?

Where did the wishing go?

Even thoughts I could not help but see
that in order to be free as the night
the hurt must grow tight and alive
as a wire in a hive of bees.

Would you please tell me:

Where did the wishing go?

Or how did I come to lose
the childish news of the dreaming,
the crystal gaze seeming to dissolve
my sorry resolve in living
and clinging to fruit trees:

I stand stinging with their smell
of rotten memory that fell with apples
down.

What name do I climb as a tree
to claim my essential heart
that lonely part as free and steady
as twilight's heady pouring
swollen into morning, until
again to starry night
it will carry me golden:

until bold then,

I will seek the bright and singing sky.

The Woolen Mill Ruin

Into the past—into the moment,
through the eyes of the woolen mill ruin,
I see through windows succinct and filled with sky,
seeing all, seeing nothing absolute.

Sheltered by this mortared patchwork of stone,
bullfrogs have been known to flourish here.
Ask the elderberry as she sips
the quicksilver veins of water at her feet.

Water lilies tremble with the weight
of decision to float or sink;
the desire for sunlight is stronger
than the cool pull of death from below.

I could drown in this wet land
and not miss life
outside these cloistered walls;
I would sing with the ringing of fluid memory.

I, too, burned to the ground,
my boards devoured by the flame of youth.
It is all lost to these leaves of maple smiling green
as we speak the beauty of fallen archways.

Once in the mortar of our mortality,
so soon the stone heaves to the stream,
it shudders like a wounded bear, rolls over one last
time.

These windows are angelic in their cloudiness,
I have spun this wool in my own ruin,
And still hear the clatter of the mill in my bones,
Feel the wool in my breath.

Wild Leeks

I harvest the wild leeks of my life,
the soil is rich and deep in my life.
Sturdy root of onion,
delicate stem of pink and green,
the leeks are the bodies of memory.

Soil rich and deep in my life,
youth and wisdom all in one hand,
the leeks are the bodies of memory,
when I knew my life would never end.

Youth and wisdom all in one hand,
now I see the earth's seduction.
Once I knew my life would never end,
but now the cool earth beckons.

Listen softly as the leeks are pulled,
sturdy root of onion,
delicate stem of pink and green.
Silence is bless-ed among the many
as I harvest the wild leeks of my life.

Bats Trilogy

1.

Daybreak,
my mother stretches her arm
freckled with copper light
to touch the branch,
a magic wand,
to the toes of the bat,
soggy and sapped
a waterlogged aviator.

The wizened old man
clings like a leaf to a beech tree
in Winter's extreme,
a paper kite,
butterfly of fur,
his drooping visage
hangs sadly out to dry.

The baton waved to the oak,
the dry mother of all poor creatures,
and my mother
dries her hands
along her thighs
and sighs.

Another child
finds his home in the wild
open arms of trees
waiting for loving airs
to bear it skyward
on the back of the night.

2.

Dusk,
my grandmother waves the garden hose,
a snake in a bed of roses
redder than the blood of saints.
She's the kind of woman
who spins gold from yarn
and slays dragons
with the Lord's Prayer.
The roses sip and rinse their velvet lips.
Evening crouches:
a cat
black and starry-eyed.

First star I see tonight,
I wish I may, I wish I might,
have this wish, I wish tonight.

Diving,
the cat of the night air tenses,
flashes her paucity of kindness.
Shutters of flying mice
chase the Cheshire cat of moon
smiling her invisible rendezvous
with Orion and his hunters.

Watch out, they'll nest in your hair!

That's what she says,
and I believe her.
I still fight the urge to cut my hair
in sirocco summer,

when bats,
strong and dry as gulls,
flap their night guard
and worry the heavens with their glee.

3.

Always,
legends of bats reside
on ledges of dripping slate.
Cavern-chilled,
they suckle their young
like other mothers,
with warm-blooded breasts.

Blind to the short-comings
of offspring
who will fly
away from home,
in Saturn's time
and not a moment before.

To pursue lofty philosophies:
Camus.
Death without dying,
living without trying,
a flight pattern wondrous
and extra-terrestrial
in its pathology of passion.

Adolescence claims
the bones of young men:

aviators of night excursions
with appetites for hanging around,
shooting the breeze
and grand-standing.

Aerial pursuits,
only a mother
of blind perfection
would not risk
the insect flight
of a child's night passages.

Blue Moon

Supposed to be blue,
this moon—
hovering on the brink
of October
fully clothed in orange
regalia.

She charges the night's maelstrom
of stars—
kindling their embers
with a tiger's glint-eyed
malice.

She's warm alright,
but don't be fooled—
beneath her crinoline
of summer gold,
a cool, watery moon
floats in satisfaction.

A smile for the dead
and other lonely dreams
of winter to come.

Solstice Moon

Blood orange.
Planetary placenta.

Not a moon at all.

More like an embryo
rising from the amniotic fluid
of stars falling—
falling stars through space.

Rising—
rising red and furious,
a volcano
branding the honor
of night's dressing gown,
a dancing flame
forged in the heart of Salome.

What pageantry it reveals
in the drama of this night
of shooting stars and Arizona winds
let out of some canyon box
all at once, in one swirling caress
of a hot lover,
gentle but persistent.

My skin alive with stars,
the wind,
my seduction.

And the red solstice moon,
the apple of Woman
here to devour
in the desert of Eden.

Birds Can Tell Time

Birds can tell time:

Their bodies sing the seasons
through down and pluming feathers,
adrift on wayward winds,
beckoning another round
of stars and avalanches.

They circle dance
through globe marshes,
rainforest and river valley
to rest in the heavens,
to plummet to the rocks
of ancient beginnings,
flounder in the sea of sky.

The message scores their bones

Flashing in neon
crystal gongs in inner ears,
they honk a winter warning,
or quicken spring fever
they frenzy in avian blood.

Gathering flocks
of flying timepieces
In sweet unison,
birds wrap the world in colored bands,
leaping through time warps,
fishing along the way,
egg-rolling,

weaving homesteads in the rushes,
tripping the light fantastic
in Arctic electric storms.

They trace the migration
of Columbus and Magellan,
with endless calculations
to light like clockwork
on one steady pond.

The Ghost Deer

This night,
He does not see Her
as He and I walk together,
nor do I see Her,
this time.

As if,
the maleness of Him
keeps Her at bay
and dissolves her flesh.

Every evening
before this,
I have spoken to Her
by full moon and wane.

In a world not of our doing,
we, doe and woman,
have shared this grazing solitaire,
on those nights
when neither man nor buck
dared to strut from the tree line,
leer or lower his horns.

We, doe and woman,
alone, but together,
in our clarity of thought and scent,
have echoed the beauty
of each other's sadness:
the fine-boned desire
to linger long in the wetness,

smell the grass
matted to our haunches
as we span the length of our singular meadow.

Fairytales and Frogs

Fairytales are like frogs,
leaping for the lust of it,
creeping through the dust of it,
the horror close behind.

Who knows the shame
in stalking the fairies,
and our children,
our polliwogs.

Remember clouds over Hiroshima,
when that great red sun
bowled its oranges over
like spilt milk of nursery rhyme?

Remember locust over Oklahoma,
when frogs fell like gray rain from the sky,
cool-whipped by weather gone awry
portending of crisp Midwestern corn.

Remember fires over Arizona,
When young men fried like frogs
Huddled in foiled skillets
Nature fanning her burning skirt.

The tempest comes to us slowly,
lonely as a cyclone of dust
in a fairytale.

What are Tears?

What is this thing called tears?
Why the tears?

What purpose to fill up one's eyes
over-spill and sop up the wet
thereafter, is there a hereafter?

What are tears?
There is nothing in my eye.
So why cry?

Moving water through aqueducts,
is not the canal a full place already?

Why not stars shooting out?
Why not frogs croaking forth?
Is the dormouse still racing against a tide of tears?

What song is this poured down my cheeks?
The light lost, or the light found?

Is it just a backup to fullness,
the dam release necessary to sing the body,
clarity to clear the body?

Ground-up mysteries
that require the light of day?

To cry like a baby is to cradle yourself
the dark wall standing guard

This is what tears are:
The interface between light and dark.
The river of light bursting to be free
as a waterfall.

Sadness is Like an Old Friend

Sadness is like an old friend.
It clings to the ribs
Where heart meets flesh,
the wasteland of trivia—
times lost and found—
irretrievable
Samurai of the spirit.

The Chamber

"Phoebe Johnson colored girl died in hope of Christ Aug. 31, 1832, aged 22." —Gravestone, Windsor, Vermont

The chamber's air is close with the must
of others gone before her,
those who traveled the night
by Orion's light
and the dipper's icy finger.

Her eyes are old as the moon,
but with the lungs of a new mother,
She trains her breath
to siphon the waning air
caught between the wings of moths.

Dusk reaches to dawn;
steam rises from her chocolate arms,
breasts bulging in the nest of her bosom,
they long to suckle her other child
lost in the chamber of her womb.

The milky way cannot compete
with the wet torture
of her weeping body:
sweat and milk spilling like sap
from a sweet black birch.

The chamber walls weep
crying in underground springs,
seep into the trap of her soft flesh
blackening the earthen floor with blood.

One bold child punctures the light
between earth and body,
drowning the moths in opal rain
and the air is sucked bone-dry as clay.

On their own taut wings,
mother and child fly
to the northern star icy and bright,
by Orion's light,
and the dipper's icy finger.

The Weight of the World

The weight of the world has shifted
to the darkness inside us all.

The wait of the world is cleaved,
and now two years hence,
the waiting we weave is our longing for joy.

Our heart opens to strangers
unmasked with the weight of light on faces
greeting another year, when waiting no longer weighs,
or irons our breath with the weight of waiting for release,
a new day unchained to fear.

The wait has been long,
but the weight can no longer weigh us down
in the darkness of a world lightweight and unsung.

Yo Duermo, un Gato

Yo duermo, un gato
todo sangre caliente.
Yo sueño a los peces simpaticos.
Aquí está el cielo en la tierra.

¿Pero, dónde está la Esperanza
en la pescar sin el
agua clara
de tu espirtu,
y en la muerte de los
momentos,
tienes en dos manos
un corazon derramandose?

Esta vida está madura con
cancion
en el sueño de tus huesos
huesos
como tu despiertas
el santuario de los peces
de colores
de el cuenco que guardas
en tu ventana.

Yo duermo, un gato
todo sangre caliente
Yo sueño a los peces simpaticos
tu guardas el silente cuenco
de tu vida.

I Sleep, a Cat

I sleep, a cat
all warm-blooded.
I dream of friendly fish.
Here is heaven on earth.

Where is the hope
in fishing without the
clear water
of your spirit?
and in the death of the
moments
you hold in two hands
in one heart?

This life is ripe with
song
in the slumber of your
bones
as you awaken
the sanctuary of the
goldfish
of the bowl you keep in
your window.

I sleep, a cat
all warm-blooded.
I dream of friendly fish
you keep in the silent bowl
of your life.

Stars

Stars,
light my way
to sleep.

I dare not
go alone
into the night
of hidden worlds.

When quiet
is a whisper
and dawn
comes too quickly.

Acknowledgments

The poet and publisher would like to thank *The Larcom Review* and the *Anthology of New England Writers* for publishing her work. "Dreaming of Apples" was first published in *Vermont Life Magazine,* winner of the Ralph Nadding Hill Literary Award for 2012.